✳ Smithsonian

LITTLE EXPLORER

Matter

by Megan Cooley Peterson

raintree 🌿
a Capstone company — publishers for children

Raintree is an imprint of Capstone Global Library Limited, a company incorporated in England and Wales having its registered office at 264 Banbury Road, Oxford, OX2 7DY – Registered company number: 6695582

www.raintree.co.uk
myorders@raintree.co.uk

Edited by Michelle Parkin
Designed by Kyle Grenz
Original illustrations © Capstone Global Library Limited 2020
Picture research by Eric Gohl
Production by Tori Abraham
Originated by Capstone Global Library Ltd
Printed and bound in India

978 1 4747 8707 9 (hardback)
978 1 4747 8712 3 (paperback)

British Library Cataloguing in Publication Data
A full catalogue record for this book is available from the British Library.

Acknowledgements
We would like to thank the following for permission to reproduce photographs: Science Source: David M. Phillips, 7; Shutterstock: 123dartist, 19 (bottom), Alesia Kan, 4, Alexey Repka, 23 (left), Alta Oosthuizen, 29 (bottom), Anastasiia Craft, 19 (bark), AR Images, 24, Billion Photos, cover (middle), Chen Peng, 19 (blocks), CHIARI VFX, cover (top), corbac40, 9, COULANGES, 19 (dolphin), danylyukk1, 27 (inset), Designua, 25, Evannovostro, background (throughout), Evgeny Drablenkov, 14, George Rudy, 21, Jef Wodniack, 5, Jezper, cover (bottom), Jeroen Mikkers, 19 (ducklings), Kuzmenko Viktoria, 26, Lesterman, 19 (soup), Magdalena Kucova, 12, majivecka, 23 (person), Olha Yerofieieva, 8, Piotr Piatrouski, 19 (igloo), Sean Locke Photography, 10–11, Serkan Senturk, 27, snapgalleria, 6, Songchai W, 29 (top), Take Photo, 1, 15, Tarasyuk Igor, 13, TUM2282, 17 (bottom), udaix, 15 (inset), Unkas Photo, 17 (top), Vadim Sadovski, 23 (planets)

Our very special thanks to Henry D. Winter III, PhD, Astrophysicist, Center for Astrophysics, Harvard and Smithsonian. We would also like to thank Kealy Gordon, Product Development Manager, and the following at Smithsonian Enterprises: Ellen Nanney, Licensing Manager; Brigid Ferraro, Vice President, Education and Consumer Products; and Carol LeBlanc, Senior Vice President, Education and Consumer Products.

Contents

What is matter?

Look around you. Everything you see is matter. Your shoes and bed are matter. Even the house you live in is matter. The Sun, Moon and stars above you are matter too. Matter is anything that takes up space and has mass. Matter can be a solid, liquid or gas. It can be soft, hard, dry, wet, bumpy or smooth.

Man-made objects are matter. Anything that you can build or make is matter.

Animals and plants are living matter. But most matter on Earth is not alive. Rocks, metal and water are non-living matter.

Building blocks of matter

What is matter made of? All matter has atoms. Atoms are too small to see without a microscope. Living things are made of cells. Cells are made of atoms too. The human body has trillions of different types of cells. One cell has about 100 trillion atoms.

A single atom is a million times smaller than the width of a human hair.

structure of an atom

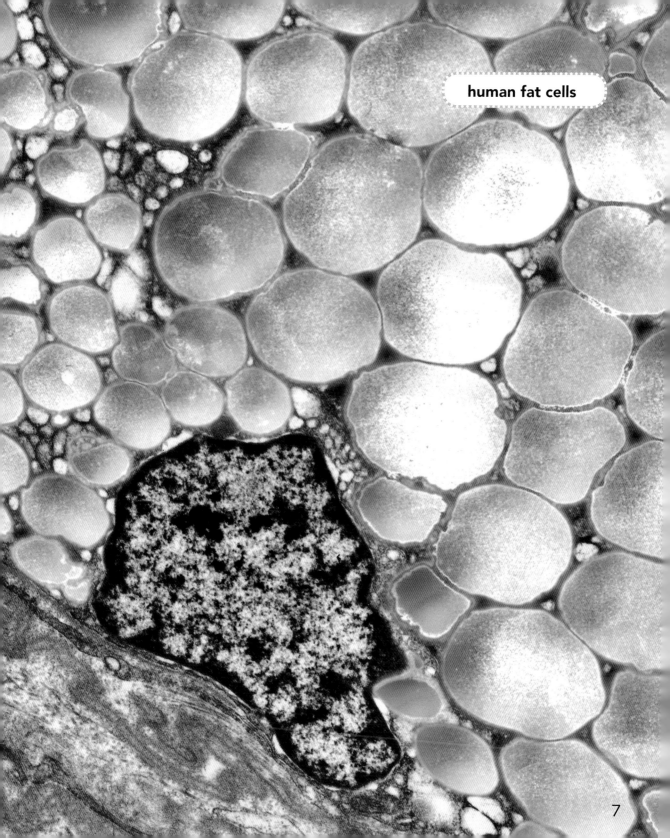

human fat cells

States of matter

The three states of matter are solids, liquids and gases. Solids hold their shape. Liquids have no shape of their own. Gases constantly change their shape.

Your body is made of all three states of matter. Your bones and muscles are solids. Your blood is liquid. Gases such as oxygen flow through your blood.

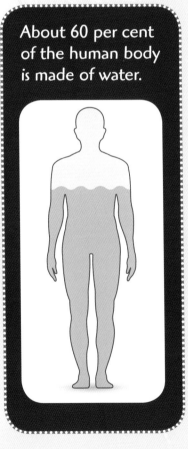

About 60 per cent of the human body is made of water.

ice

solid

water

liquid

steam

gas

9

Solids

You use solid matter every day. Your toothbrush, shoes and rucksack are all solid matter. The atoms in a solid object are bunched together. They can't move around. This is how solids keep their shape.

Not all solids act in the same way. Pull on a rubber band. It stretches. If you let it go, the band goes back to its original shape. Now try to bend a crisp. It will break in half.

Liquids

Pour water into a glass. The water takes the shape of the glass. What happens if you tip the glass upside down? The water spills out into a puddle on the floor. It doesn't hold its shape like a solid.

Water, oil and syrup are all liquids.

Liquids have no shape of their own. They take on the shape of whatever they're poured into.

13

Gases

Gas is another state of matter. The air you breathe is a gas. Air is always bumping up against you. Wave your hand quickly through the air. Can you feel the air hitting your hand?

Gases change their shape. Unlike liquids, gases completely fill whatever they're put into.

You may think that fog is a gas. But it's actually a liquid. Fog is made of tiny water droplets.

The air in a hot-air balloon makes the balloon float.

Gas atoms have a lot of space between them. They can spread out or move closer together.

gas atoms

Most gases are invisible to the human eye.

Materials

Materials are made of matter. Water, soil and wood are examples of materials. Turn on your tap. Water pours out. Dig into the soil and plant a seed. Use pieces of wood to build a tree house.

Humans use materials every day. Cotton can be made into clothing. Logs are burned for heat and light. Glass is used to make windows. Builders use steel to make skyscrapers.

Concrete is a man-made material. People use concrete to build roads, bridges and buildings.

Physical properties of matter

Matter has physical properties. A physical property is something that you can see, touch or smell. Matter can be hard or soft, heavy or light, hot or cold. A fuzzy blanket is soft. A bicycle helmet is hard.

Colour is another physical property of matter. Matter comes in all different colours. The ocean can be blue or green. The Sun is yellow. You can see through some matter such as glass and water.

Properties of matter

hot

a bowl of hot soup

hard

a cement block

smooth

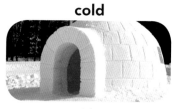

a dolphin

cold

an igloo

soft

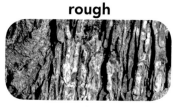

ducklings

rough

tree bark

A diamond is one of the hardest natural materials on Earth.

Density and volume

All matter has mass. Mass is the amount of matter inside an object. Objects with more mass have more density. A bowling ball has more mass than a beach ball. It's denser. Oil is less dense than water. That's why oil floats on water.

Volume is the space that matter takes up. Solids and liquids always keep the same volume when put into containers. Gas spreads out to fill whatever container it is in. Its volume changes. When you blow up a balloon, your breath fills the whole balloon.

A solid's volume is usually measured by units such as cubic centimetres (cm^3).

Mass and weight

Weight measures how hard gravity pulls down on an object. Without gravity, everything on Earth would float into space!

Mass is not the same as weight. An object's mass never changes. But its weight might. The pull of gravity is not the same on every planet. If you went to Mars, you would weigh less than you do on Earth. That's because Mars has weaker gravity.

"Remember to look up at the stars and not down at your feet. Try to make sense of what you see and wonder about what makes the universe exist. Be curious."

– physicist Stephen Hawking

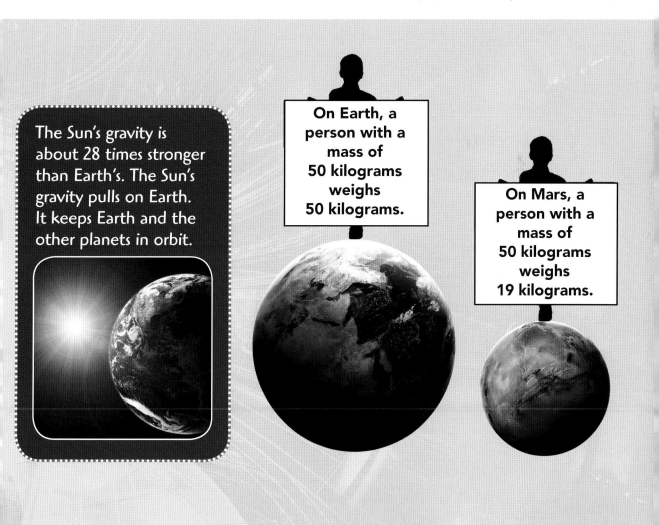

The Sun's gravity is about 28 times stronger than Earth's. The Sun's gravity pulls on Earth. It keeps Earth and the other planets in orbit.

On Earth, a person with a mass of 50 kilograms weighs 50 kilograms.

On Mars, a person with a mass of 50 kilograms weighs 19 kilograms.

Changing states of matter

Matter can change states. Have you ever eaten an ice cream on a hot summer's day? After a while the ice cream begins to melt. Why? The Sun's heat raised the air's temperature. The higher temperature turned the solid ice cream into a liquid.

Not all solids melt. When wood is heated, it turns into ash. This is a chemical change. It can't be changed back.

Some matter changes state when heat is added or taken away. Add heat to water. Eventually it boils. Some boiling water escapes into the air as a gas. This is called steam.

Changing states of matter

gas

liquid solid

Melting points of solids

chocolate	36 degrees Celsius (97 degrees Fahrenheit)
gold	1,062 degrees C (1,943 degrees F)
iron	1,510 degrees C (2,750 degrees F)

Boiling points of liquids

water at sea level	100 degrees C (212 degrees F)
household vinegar	101 degrees C (213 degrees F)
olive oil	300 degrees C (572 degrees F)

The water cycle

Rain and snow depend on the changing states of matter. For rain to form, the air fills with water vapour. The water vapour rises and cools. Then it turns into water droplets. It has changed from a gas into a liquid. The droplets form clouds in the sky. Sometimes the droplets are heavier than air. When this happens, they fall from the sky as raindrops.

Dew forms on grass when water vapour in the air loses heat.

Water cycle

clouds form

droplets are
heavier than air

rain or
snow falls

water collects
on the ground

water
vapour
rises

Mixing matter

Matter doesn't just change. It can be mixed together. Take a glass of water and some ice cubes. The solid ice cube melts into the liquid water. This causes the water to cool. The ocean is made of salt water. Salt is a solid. The salt dissolves into the ocean water, creating saltwater.

Matter matters! It is all around you. Step outside and look up. The Sun and clouds are made of matter. Now look down. The ants crawling along the pavement are made of matter. So is the pavement. There would be no life on Earth without matter.

Glossary

atom smallest part of matter

density amount of mass an object or substance has based on a unit of volume

gravity force that pulls objects together

mass amount of material in an object

microscope tool that makes very small things look large enough to be seen

orbit path an object such as a planet follows as it goes around the Sun

oxygen colourless gas that people and animals breathe; humans and animals need oxygen to live

property quality of a material, such as colour, hardness or shape

trillion 1,000 times one billion

volume amount of space taken up by an object or substance

water vapour water in gas form; water vapour is one of many invisible gases in the air

weight measurement of how heavy something is

Comprehension questions

1. What are the three states of matter?

2. Every object has mass and weight. Why is an object's weight greater on Earth than on Mars?

3. On cold days, your breath looks like a white cloud. What is happening to your breath?

Find out more

Books

All About Physics (Big Questions), Richard Hammond
(DK Children, 2015)

Knowledge Encyclopedia Science!, DK (DK Children, 2018)

The Solid Truth About States of Matter (Graphic Science), Agnieszka Biskup (Raintree, 2011)

Werewolves and States of Matter (Monster Science), Janet Slingerland
(Raintree, 2012)

Website

www.bbc.co.uk/bitesize/topics/zkgg87h/articles/zsgwwxs
Learn more about the different states of matter.

Index